T0029459

# save the . . .
# TURTLES

by **Sarah L. Thomson**
*with an introduction*
by **Chelsea Clinton**

PHILOMEL

PHILOMEL
An imprint of Penguin Random House LLC, New York

First published in the United States of America by Philomel,
an imprint of Penguin Random House LLC, 2024

Text copyright © 2024 by Chelsea Clinton

Photo credits: page 4: © U.S. National Park Service; page 6: © Yuriy Vahlenko/Adobe
Stock; page 7: © U.S. National Park Service; pages 9: © paulacobleigh/Adobe Stock;
page 11: © Diego/Adobe Stock; page 15: EcoView/Adobe Stock; page 17: © Mufti Adi/
Adobe Stock; page 19: © Aekkaphum/Adobe Stock; page 24: © mirecca/Adobe Stock;
page 28: © Darrin Henry/Adobe Stock; page 36: © Jason/Adobe Stock; page 39: © Ken
Griffiths/Adobe Stock; page 42: © Vasilii/Adobe Stock; page 48: © QuietWord/
Adobe Stock; page 52: © donyanedomam/Adobe Stock; page 54: © U.S. National Park
Service; page 60: © shellygraphy/Adobe Stock

Philomel is a registered trademark of Penguin Random House LLC.
The Penguin colophon is a registered trademark of Penguin Books Limited.

Visit us online at PenguinRandomHouse.com.

Library of Congress Cataloging-in-Publication Data is available.

ISBN 9780593623404 (hardcover)
ISBN 9780593623428 (paperback)

1st Printing

Printed in the United States of America

LSCC

Edited by Talia Benamy • Design by Lily Qian
Text set in Calisto MT Pro

# save the . . .

save the . . .
**BLUE WHALES**

save the . . .
**PANDAS**

save the . . .
**ELEPHANTS**

save the . . .
**PENGUINS**

save the . . .
**FROGS**

save the . . .
**POLAR BEARS**

save the . . .
**GIRAFFES**

save the . . .
**RHINOCEROSES**

save the . . .
**GORILLAS**

save the . . .
**TIGERS**

save the . . .
**KOALAS**

save the . . .
**TURTLES**

save the . . .
**LIONS**

save the . . .
**WHALE SHARKS**

Dear Reader,

When I was around your age, my favorite animals were dinosaurs and elephants. I wanted to know everything I could about triceratopses, stegosauruses and other dinosaurs that had roamed our earth millions of years ago. Elephants, though, captured my curiosity and my heart. The more I learned about the largest animals on land today, the more I wanted to do to help keep them and other endangered species safe forever.

So I joined organizations working around the world to support endangered species and went to our local zoo to learn more about conservation efforts close to home (thanks to my parents and grandparents). I tried to learn as much as I could about how we can ensure animals and plants don't go extinct like the dinosaurs, especially since it's the choices that we're making that pose the greatest threat to their lives today.

The choices we make don't have to be huge to make

a real difference. When I was in elementary school, I used to cut up the plastic rings around six-packs of soda, glue them to brightly colored construction paper (purple was my favorite) and hand them out to whomever would take one in a one-girl campaign to raise awareness about the dangers that plastic six-pack rings posed to marine wildlife around the world. I learned about that from a book—*50 Simple Things Kids Can Do to Save the Earth*—which helped me understand that you're never too young to make a difference and that we all can change the world. I hope that this book will inform and inspire you to help save this and other endangered species. There are tens of thousands of species that are currently under threat, with more added every year. We have the power to save those species, and with your help, we can.

Sincerely,

Chelsea Clinton

# save the . . .
# TURTLES

# CONTENTS

----------------------------------------

# 1

## JUST ABOUT ANYWHERE: WHERE TURTLES LIVE

Scorching deserts. Vast oceans. Lush rainforests, cool woodlands, marshy wetlands, and backyard creeks. If you look hard enough, you can find a turtle almost anywhere.

You can tell a lot about where a turtle lives from the shape of its feet. A turtle with webbed feet that are good for swimming spends at least some time in the water. But it may crawl onto land now and then. A turtle with round, stumpy feet spends its entire life on dry land. This kind of land-dwelling turtle is also called a tortoise. And if a turtle has long flippers instead of feet, it's a sea (or marine) turtle. These turtles almost never leave the ocean.

There is only one continent on Earth where you won't find a turtle, and that's Antarctica. All turtles are reptiles, which means they are cold-blooded. Their body temperature is about the same as the air or water around them. They cannot survive in a place like Antarctica that has freezing temperatures year-round.

## In the Desert

If you are in the Mojave Desert or other dry places in the southwestern United States, you might be able to spot a desert tortoise. They can grow to be more than a foot long, and they survive the harsh climate they live in by digging underground burrows where they spend much of their time.

In winter months, a desert tortoise uses its burrow to wait out the cold. It barely moves. Even its lungs and heart work slowly. In this state, it uses very little energy. When a warm-blooded animal like a bear deals with cold weather in this way, it's called hibernation. When a cold-blooded animal like a tortoise does it, it's called brumation.

The desert tortoise handles the worst heat of summer much like it handles cold—by waiting it out underground, staying still and quiet. In this state, which is called estivation, the tortoise needs very little water to survive.

When the temperature is not too hot or too cold, the tortoise crawls out of its burrow,

*The fruit of the prickly pear cactus is a favorite food for the desert tortoise.*

looking for plants to eat and rainwater to drink. It moves at about one-fifth of a mile per hour. That means it would take roughly twenty minutes to walk the length of a football field. If you didn't dawdle, you could probably walk that same distance in about two minutes.

## In Freshwater

The largest North American turtle that lives in freshwater (instead of the salty ocean) is the alligator snapping turtle. The biggest males can weigh as much as a Great Dane.

Alligator snapping turtles spend almost all of their time in the water. Females crawl onto the shore only to lay their eggs.

To find food, an alligator snaping turtle may settle down on the bottom of a lake, river, or pond and open up its mouth. A bit of its tongue is bright red in color and looks like a wiggling worm. If a curious fish comes near, hoping for a meal, the turtle will snap it up with its powerful jaws.

Snapping turtles don't attack people, but it's wise to be cautious of them and never pick

*With its spiky shell and pointed beak, an alligator snapping turtle looks a bit like a dinosaur.*

them up. Those jaws can close with a force of a thousand pounds, which is about six times more powerful than the average human bite.

## In Woods or Meadows

In the forests and grasslands of the eastern United States, from Florida to Illinois and as far north as Maine, you may come across an eastern box turtle. The yellow-orange markings on its dark brown shell help this small turtle stay hidden among fallen leaves. Eastern box turtles eat whatever they come across, including fruit, insects, eggs, and dead animals.

*An eastern box turtle spends most of its time on land but is still considered a turtle, not a tortoise.*

## On an Island

Off the coast of Ecuador, you can find a Galapagos tortoise—actually thirteen kinds of Galapagos tortoises. Each kind, or species, dwells on its own island, and each is a little different from the others.

All Galapagos tortoises (which are also called giant tortoises) are plant-eaters. All are large, nearly five feet in length. They would just about fit in a child's wading pool. Most adult males weigh more than five hundred pounds. There are two main types: dome-shelled and saddlebacked.

Dome-shelled Galapagos tortoises have shells with a simple curved shape. They tend to live on large, humid islands where plenty of plant life grows.

Saddlebacked tortoises mostly live on smaller, drier islands. They have a curve or a dip in the

*Most tortoises have tall, domed shells, like these two Galapagos tortoises.*

front of the shell where the tortoise's head comes out. This dip allows the tortoise to stretch its neck up higher than its dome-shelled relatives so it can reach more kinds of food.

## In the Ocean

In the ocean, you can find seven species of sea turtles. Their long, flat flippers make them powerful swimmers. The front flippers pull them through the water, and the back flippers act like rudders, steering the turtles where they want to go.

Sea turtles can't spend their entire lives underwater the way that fish do. They must come up to the surface to breathe. But they don't have to do it very often. When resting, a sea turtle can hold its breath for four to seven hours! Most species can dive up to nine hundred feet when they are hunting for prey. The largest sea turtle of all, the leatherback, is able to dive deeper than any of its relatives—more than three thousand feet below the surface of the water. That's twice as deep as the Empire State Building is tall!

Like all turtles, leatherbacks are cold-blooded, but even so, they can swim and dive in very cold ocean water. This is partly because of the large muscles that make up their big bodies. These muscles create a lot of heat as the turtle swims, keeping it from freezing. The dark colors of its shell also help this turtle soak up heat from the sun.

*A leatherback hatchling starts out tiny but will grow up to weigh hundreds, and perhaps even thousands, of pounds.*

Whether they swim in icy ocean waters, doze in desert burrows, or bask in steamy swamps, all turtles have some things in common. The most obvious, of course, is their shell.

## LIFE INSIDE A SHELL:
## WHAT TURTLES ARE LIKE

Many animals have hard shells that cover and protect the soft bodies inside. Think of insects like beetles and ants, crustaceans like lobsters and crabs, or mollusks like clams, scallops, and mussels.

But turtles are different from other shelled creatures in one important way: they have a backbone. This means they are a type of animal called a vertebrate. Humans, dogs, mice, monkeys, alligators, snakes, fish, and birds are all vertebrates as well.

In the world of vertebrates, only two creatures have shells: the turtle (the only shelled reptile) and the armadillo (the only shelled mammal).

A turtle shell has two parts. The top part is the carapace, and the bottom is the plastron.

Both the carapace and plastron are made of bones—between fifty-nine and sixty-one of them. These bones are joined together with a layer of flat plates called scutes. Scutes are formed from keratin, which is what your fingernails are made of. If you stroke a turtle's shell, it's the scutes you are touching.

Because the shell is part of a turtle's skeleton, it cannot crawl out of it. The shell goes with the animal wherever it goes. And a turtle can feel pressure and pain through the shell, just as you can feel pressure if you push on your fingernail.

Some species of turtle can pull their heads entirely inside their shells. These are called hidden-neck turtles. Some have to let out the air in their lungs to make room, which means

*All tortoises (like this leopard tortoise) are part of the hidden-neck group.*

they hiss as they hide inside their shells.

Other turtles can't retreat completely into their shells. But some can tuck their head sideways along the edge of their shell to protect it. These are called side-necked turtles.

And sea turtles can't pull their heads into their shells at all.

No matter whether it can hide a turtle's head or not, the shell is good protection. Most turtles can't move fast, but they don't really need to. The tough surface of their shells keeps most predators from trying to take a bite.

But shells can also put turtles in danger. You'll learn more about this in chapter three.

## Starting from an Egg

Like most reptiles, turtles hatch from eggs. Some turtles lay eggs with hard shells. Others

*This snake-necked turtle shows how a side-necked turtle hides its head.*

lay eggs with shells that are a little soft but tough, almost leathery to the touch.

After she lays her eggs, a mother turtle will bury them under sand, soil, or plants. Once the eggs have been hidden, most females leave them alone to hatch when they are ready.

Only one species will stay with a nest to guard it—the Asian giant tortoise. This tortoise lives in the warm, damp forests and rainforests of South Asian countries like India, Bangladesh, and Thailand. A female will snap at any predators that come near her nest. She may also crouch over her nest to protect the eggs underneath.

While turtle eggs, no matter the species, are under the ground, something remarkable happens. Inside the egg, the babies develop as male or female depending on the temperature of the sand, soil, or plants that cover them.

If the temperature is around 82°F, roughly half the hatchlings will be male and half will be female. If the temperature is warmer than 82°, most or all will be female. Cooler temperatures mean most or all will be male. (The same thing happens to baby alligators and crocodiles.)

When the hatchlings are ready to live on their own, they break through their shells. A bump on their beaks called a caruncle helps them chop their way out. Then they crawl or scramble out of the nest.

*A young tortoise makes its way out of its shell.*

A newly hatched turtle has a soft shell that cannot protect it very well. It may easily become a tasty meal for a predator like a shark, alligator, seabird, fox, crab, raccoon, dog, or human being.

That means hatchlings who live on land scramble to hide under plants or in fallen leaves. Water-dwelling turtles hurry as fast as they can to the nearest ocean, lake, river, or marsh. They can swim away from predators faster than they can crawl.

If it escapes being eaten, a hatchling will quickly have to find something to eat for itself.

## What Do Turtles Eat?

It depends on the species. Some are herbivores, or plant-eaters. This includes most tortoises. Leaves, grass, algae, cactus pads, flowers, and fruits can all become a tasty meal.

Others are meat-eaters, or carnivores, and hunt for their prey. Most snapping turtles hunt fish, frogs, snakes, and even small birds. Leatherback turtles eat jellyfish, along with a squid now and then.

And many turtles are omnivores, eating both plants and meat. Green sea turtles start life as omnivores, munching sea grass and also hunting for worms, water-dwelling insects, fish eggs, and young crustaceans, like crabs. Later, when the hatchlings grow into adults, they become plant-eaters, dining on seagrass and algae.

No matter what it eats, a turtle doesn't use teeth to chew. That's because it doesn't have any! Instead, it has a hard beak like a bird's to chop off chunks of food and swallow them whole. But turtles that eat hard-shelled mollusks such as clams or oysters do have a ridge on the roof of their mouths that they can use to crush their prey before they gulp it down.

Eating gives hatchlings the energy they need to grow to their adult size. Some adult turtles are small enough to fit easily in your hand. The tiny speckled tortoise (also called the speckled padloper) doesn't grow to be more than four inches. The largest turtle of all, the leatherback, grows to have a shell that is six feet long, bigger than the hoods of most cars.

Once they are full-grown adults, it's time for a female turtle to mate, dig a nest, and lay her own eggs. Some are ready to do this when they are two or three years old. Other species must wait ten or fifteen years, or even more. It can take a green sea turtle anywhere from twenty-four to forty years before she's old enough to lay eggs.

And some turtles must make an incredibly difficult journey before egg-laying can begin.

## Amazing Migrations

Sea turtles spend their lives in the ocean, and many of them swim long distances searching for food. Every two or three years, adults return to the water near the beaches where they were hatched.

If a female is ready to lay her own eggs, she will make her way out of the ocean and dig a nest in the sand. Egg-laying is the only time she will come ashore in her adult life. Males make the long journey along with females, but they do not crawl out of the water. Once a male hatchling enters the ocean, he never leaves it again.

Some sea turtles must swim for hundreds or even thousands of miles to make this migration. There are green sea turtles that nest in the Ascension Islands of Canada but feed in the warmer oceans off Brazil. They must travel over 1,200 miles between these two places.

There are also loggerhead turtles that nest on the beaches of Florida. Once their eggs have been laid, they return to the water, where they may be carried as far north as Maine by the Gulf Stream. Some even cross the Atlantic to Europe. In time, they swim back to warmer waters to begin the process once more.

Leatherback turtles are the champions

*Some loggerhead turtles must cross an entire ocean to lay their eggs.*

of migration. These long-distance swimmers are found in the Atlantic, Pacific, and Indian Oceans, and also in the Mediterranean Sea. They are known to swim as far north as Canada and Norway, and as far south as New Zealand. On average, a leatherback swims 3,700 miles (one way!) between the waters where it hunts for food and the beaches where a female lays her eggs.

How can a turtle find its way through thousands of miles of ocean to arrive at the beach where it was born? Scientists call this process "natal homing," and it is still mysterious. But sea turtles have a sense that humans don't have, and it may help them on their migrations.

When you hold a compass in your hand, you can watch the needle spin until it points north. This happens because the compass's needle is a magnet, and so is the planet Earth.

Every magnet has two ends or poles—a north and a south. The north pole of one magnet attracts the south pole of another. (And the opposite also happens—the north pole of one magnet will repel, or push away, the north pole of another magnet.)

This is what happens to the magnet inside the compass and the magnet that is the Earth. The south pole of the needle is pulled toward the north pole of the Earth's magnetic field, which happens to be near the planet's North Pole. That's why a compass needle always points north.

Humans cannot sense the Earth's magnetic field. But it seems that sea turtles can. It's like they have a built-in compass in their heads, helping them find their way.

Leatherbacks also have another sense that may help. On its head, each turtle has a pink spot. (It looks a little different on each turtle.) The skin over this spot is thin. Sunlight reaches through the pink skin and into a part of the brain that is sensitive to light and dark.

As Earth moves through the seasons, days become longer in summer and shorter in winter. The pink spot may help leatherbacks sense these changes and may give a female turtle a hint that it is time to start swimming back to warmer water and to the right beach to lay her eggs.

## Long, Long Life Spans

Once it has hatched, a turtle may live for just a few years—or for many decades. It's common for turtles to live twenty or thirty years. Large sea turtles may survive up to sixty or seventy or even more.

And then there's Jonathan.

Jonathan, a Seychelles giant tortoise, lives on the island of Saint Helena, which is in the southern Atlantic Ocean. He spends his days in the lawns and gardens of Plantation House, the mansion where the governor of the island lives. And he is the oldest living land animal on Earth. (There are some ocean-dwelling animals that are older. Scientists recently encountered a Greenland shark that is four hundred years old and a clam that had lived to five hundred.)

In 1882, Jonathan was given as a gift to the man who would become governor of St. Helena. He was already an adult tortoise at the time. It's believed that he hatched in the 1830s, which would make him more than 190 years old today.

One reason that Jonathan and other turtles can survive so long is that their bodies don't seem to age the way human bodies do. People (and other mammals) have bodies that slowly wear out, year by year, as they get older. This

*Jonathan the Seychelles giant tortoise hatched before the American Civil War broke out, before the light bulb was invented, and before the first game of basketball was played.*

doesn't seem to happen to turtles. Once they reach adulthood, their bodies change very little as the years go by.

Turtles are not completely protected from old age. Their hearts, as well as their eyesight, do start to wear out near the end of their lives. But it can take a very long time for this to happen, especially if a turtle lives in a zoo (or in the gardens of a governor's mansion), with lots of food to eat and at a comfortable temperature all year round. Scientists are still studying turtles, trying to learn more about how and why they live so long.

Not all turtles are as lucky as Jonathan, who has lived for almost two centuries. All around the world, turtles are facing threats that make it difficult for them to survive.

# 3

# PLASTIC, HUNTING, AND GLOBAL WARMING: WHY TURTLES ARE ENDANGERED

The International Union for Conservation of Nature (or IUCN) keeps track of animal species all over the world. Its IUCN Red List of Threatened Species™ puts animals into seven different categories:

**Least Concern:** This animal is doing all right. There are enough healthy animals to have enough healthy babies to keep the species going.

**Near Threatened:** This animal is not in

trouble yet, but there are danger signs. It may become Vulnerable, Endangered, or Critically Endangered soon.

**Vulnerable:** There are not many of this animal left. Its numbers are falling, and it can live only in certain small areas. It is at risk of extinction.

**Endangered:** This animal is at high risk of extinction.

**Critically Endangered:** This animal is at very high risk of extinction.

**Extinct in the Wild:** This animal lives only in captivity. There are none left in the wild.

**Extinct:** This animal is gone forever.

There are about 350 species of turtle and tortoise in the world today. Some are of Least Concern. But others, like the alligator snapping turtle or the many different kinds of Galapagos tortoise, are at risk. About half the world's species of turtle are Threatened. One-third are Critically Endangered.

What is making life so hard for turtles and tortoises?

## A Place to Live

Like any animal, turtles need a habitat—somewhere they can find food, water, and shelter. They also need a chance to meet with others of their species so that they can find mates and lay eggs.

But habitats are getting harder and harder to find. When people take up land to build farms, houses, stores, factories, roads, sidewalks, and railroad tracks, there is less space left for turtles and other wild animals.

On the southern tip of South Africa, you'll

find the only habitat where the geometric tortoise can live. It eats plants that only grow in this area.

But 90 percent of this tortoise's habitat has been used by humans, mostly as farms. There is only one-tenth left wild for the geometric star tortoise to find a home in. It is now Critically Endangered and one of the rarest tortoises in the world.

Turtles who depend on beaches as part of their habitat are also in trouble all over the world. People love to build houses and hotels near the water. It's wonderful to live or go on vacation right next to a beach where you can play and swim. But if too many people are using a beach, it will be hard for sea turtles to lay eggs there.

People often build walls and jetties to protect their homes from waves and high tides. These barriers can block turtles from crawling ashore. Trampling feet or the wheels of bikes, cars, and off-road vehicles can break buried eggs or pack down sand so that turtles can't dig nests.

Houses, stores, hotels, and roads come with another danger to sea turtles—lights. Hatchlings usually break out of their shells at night, and they head toward the brightest light they see. Most of the time, this is the moon glowing on the ocean, and it leads the baby turtles where they need to be.

Streetlights, car lights, and neon signs can confuse the hatchlings. If they crawl in the wrong direction, they may become lost, tired, and too weak to reach the water. Or they may end up on a road where they could be crushed by cars.

All of these dangers mean fewer young sea

*Lights like these could easily lure a hatchling away from the water.*

turtles make it safely to the water, and fewer will return to the beach to lay eggs of their own.

## Food and Pets

If you were hungry and hunting for some food, a turtle would be pretty easy to catch. They can't run fast. The shell that protects them from most predators won't stop a human who wants a meal.

People have been using turtles as food for thousands of years. There were once giant tortoises in Florida, but they don't exist today. They were probably hunted to extinction. When humans first arrived on the island of Madagascar, they killed off the giant tortoises there as well.

From the 1600s to the 1800s, merchants, whalers, and pirates took giant tortoises from the Galapagos Islands. The tortoises were stored alive on their ships, turned upside down so that they could not escape. They survived without food or water for months before being killed and cooked for the crew. The Galapagos probably lost between one hundred thousand and two hundred thousand tortoises from this cruel trade.

Today, people all over the world continue to

use turtles and their eggs as sources of food. And they also hunt them because they think that their bones, shells, blood, and body parts can be used as medicine. There is no evidence that this actually works, but many people still think it's true.

Chinese three-striped box turtles were once common in Asia—but not anymore. This is partly because some people think that their shells can cure cancer. (Just to be clear—they can't. A turtle shell isn't real medicine.) But because of this belief, there are places where a single Chinese three-striped box turtle can be sold for thousands of dollars. These turtles are now Critically Endangered.

Others take turtles from the wild to keep or sell as pets. People who do this don't always care that they are breaking rules about selling wild animals. By doing so, they make it harder and harder for many species to survive.

The shells that protect turtles from predators may actually put them in more danger when people are looking for animals to take home. The Indian star tortoise, for example, is a popular pet. People who admire the lovely patterns on its shell may not even know that the star

*The pretty patterns of an Indian star tortoise make it a prized pet—which is a problem for the species.*

tortoise is considered Vulnerable or that more than fifty thousand of these tortoises are sold illegally every year.

Hunting, capturing, killing, and selling wild turtles as food, medicine, or pets means that there are fewer and fewer left in the wild where they are meant to be.

## Plastic Pollution

Even turtles that are lucky enough to live in the wild still face problems caused by humans. One of those problems is plastic.

Plastic is useful, lightweight, and water-proof. It doesn't break like glass. It weighs less than metal. And so people use it for every-thing from bottles to bags to fishing nets to toys to Styrofoam cups. (Styrofoam is a form of plastic.)

The main problem with all this? Plastic doesn't decompose, or break down, the way an apple core or an animal bone or a piece of paper does. Those things will, after time, rot away and become part of the soil.

Plastic doesn't do this. It just stays plastic. Pretty much every piece of plastic that has ever been made still exists today. It may be broken, buried, melted, left floating in the ocean, or recycled into something else made of plastic—but it's still here. (One recent study did find that some plastics can be broken down by sunlight. This may be good news—except that a lot of plastic waste is buried or deep in the ocean, where sunlight will never reach it.)

Some plastic gets recycled or reused, but a lot becomes trash. Some of that trash ends up in the ocean, where sea turtles and other animals may see it. A plastic bag drifting through the water looks a lot like a jellyfish, and a turtle may try to eat it. Some leatherback turtles, who live mainly on jellyfish, have been found with as much as eleven pounds of plastic packed into their stomachs. A turtle with a stomach full of plastic can't digest the food it actually needs to survive.

*Without help, a turtle is unlikely to be able to free itself from a plastic bag, which can slow the turtle down or even cut off its breath.*

Fishing lines and nets made of plastic also end up in the ocean when they break. These drifting strands of plastic can snag on a turtle's legs, neck, or shell. This is called entanglement.

If an entangled turtle can't free itself, the nets or lines may slow it down, cut into its skin, or even make it impossible for the turtle to swim up to the surface to breathe. A sea turtle that can't reach the surface will drown. Entanglement kills around a thousand turtles a year.

## Turtle Eggs in a Warming World

The Earth is surrounded by a layer of air: our atmosphere. The atmosphere not only provides the oxygen we need to breathe—it also helps keep our planet warm enough for life to survive here.

But there's a problem.

When human beings burn fuels like gasoline, oil, natural gas, and coal, we add a gas called carbon dioxide to the atmosphere. The more carbon dioxide that goes into the Earth's atmosphere, the warmer the planet gets. Other gases, like methane, do the same thing.

A slowly warming planet is a challenge for many kinds of wildlife. It can make it hard for animals to find enough water to drink. It can kill the plants they need to eat. It can change the time females lay eggs or have babies, which may mean young animals struggle to survive.

This type of change to Earth's climate is particularly dangerous for turtles.

That's because the temperature of the sand or soil or plant life around their eggs decides what sex the hatchlings will be. Warmer temperatures mean more females and fewer males. So when those females grow up and are ready to lay eggs, it will be harder for them to find males to mate with. Fewer eggs will be laid and fewer young turtles will be born.

It's already happening to some species. Near the northern parts of Australia's Great Barrier Reef, the green sea turtles that are hatching are almost all female. Only 1 percent are male. This species is already Endangered. Having so few males means it will be even harder for green sea turtles to avoid extinction.

So many things that people do can cause harm to turtles—throwing away a plastic bag, buying a wild turtle as a pet, using fuels that make the planet warmer. But people are also trying hard to make a better world for turtles everywhere.

# 4

## SCIENTISTS, VOLUNTEERS, AND KIDS: WHO HAS BEEN SAVING TURTLES?

Creating a world where turtles can survive means making sure that they have safe habitats, clean water, enough food, and freedom from those who hunt them.

### Tomas Diagne and the Homeland of Turtles

One of the people working to be sure that turtles have all these things is Tomas Diagne.

Tomas grew up in Dakar, Senegal. When he was a teenager, he filled up his home with creatures that needed a safe place to live: dogs and chicks along with a venomous snake. His father wasn't pleased, but he agreed to let the animals stay as long as Tomas took care of them.

Tomas became more and more interested in one particular animal: the sulcata tortoise, also called the African spurred tortoise. These huge tortoises (the third largest in the world) can grow as heavy as two hundred pounds. When he found sick or injured sulcatas, Tomas brought them home to care for.

As an adult, Tomas continued his efforts to save sulcata tortoises. His hard work won him an impressive honor: the Rolex Award for Enterprise. With the money that came with the award, he founded the Village des Tortues

*The sulcata tortoise is just one of the many species Tomas Diagne is working to save.*

(which is French for "Turtle Village"), a sanctuary for many different species of turtles and tortoises that are injured or need a safe place to live. Some spend their lives there, while others are cared for and then released back into the wild.

Tomas went on to found the African Chelonian Institute. This organization works to protect all forty-six species of turtle and tortoise in Africa. Workers there breed captive turtles and tortoises, work to save their habitats, and teach as many people as possible why these animals need protection.

The continent of Africa, Tomas often tells people, is the homeland of turtles and tortoises. All of them alive today are descended from a single species called *Eunotosaurus africanus*, which once lived where South Africa is now. By dedicating his life to protecting, saving, and educating others about turtles, Tomas hopes that these animals will continue to thrive in Senegal and all over Africa for years to come.

## Diego (and Male Number Three)

As the 1950s came to an end, Galapagos tortoises were close to extinction. This was partly because they had been hunted by sailors for centuries. And humans had created another problem for the tortoises by bringing new animals to the Galapagos.

People brought horses to ride, cows and goats to milk, pigs to use for food, and dogs and cats as pets or working animals. They also brought rats, though they didn't mean to. Rats often sneak aboard human ships looking for food, and some of the rodents made their way ashore to the Galapagos Islands.

Rats and pigs eat tortoise eggs. Horses and cows trample tortoise nests. Goats eat the same plants that tortoises need. Dogs sometimes attack and kill hatchlings and even adult tortoises. Since these animals were new to the Galapagos, the tortoises didn't know how to defend themselves or their nests.

In 1959, the government of Ecuador made almost all the Galapagos Islands into a national park. The rules of the park are very strict. All visitors must go with a guide and stick to the paths to avoid trampling food plants and destroying the habitat that tortoises and other animals need.

The government also set up the Charles Darwin Research Station in the park, named after an English scientists from the 1800s whose work changed the way we understand the natural world. Workers there began collecting tortoise eggs. The eggs were watched and protected carefully. When they hatched, the young tortoises were released only once they were old enough and big enough to give them a good chance of surviving attacks by dogs, cats, or rats.

*At the Charles Darwin Research Station, scientists work to save the unique environment of the Galápagos Islands.*

But collecting enough eggs was difficult, partly because there were not very many wild tortoises left to lay them. Some species, like the Española giant tortoise, were in particular danger. By the 1970s, there were only fifteen of these tortoises alive. (Española Island is also called Hood Island, so the species is sometimes known as the Hood Island giant tortoise.)

The San Diego Zoo had an Española Island tortoise named Diego. They sent him to the Charles Darwin Research Station in the hopes that he could help save his species.

Over the years, Diego became the father of somewhere between seven and eight hundred baby turtles. Another Española Island tortoise, who is simply known as "Male Number Three," fathered a similar number of hatchlings. But he never became as famous as Diego.

Most Galapagos tortoises are still in danger—including Española Island giant tortoises. They are on the Red List as Critically Endangered. But thanks to Diego, Male Number Three, and the scientists and researchers at the Charles Darwin Research Station, they have a chance to avoid extinction.

## Turtle Patrols

At daybreak on a spring or summer beach, you might spot some people walking along the high tide line. They're not just enjoying the sunrise. They're looking for sea turtle tracks.

During nesting season, volunteer turtle patrols check their section of beach every morning. If they find tracks, they follow them

*Tracks like these can lead to a turtle's nest.*

to the spot where churned-up sand shows that a sea turtle has been digging her nest.

Other volunteers walk the beaches at night, which is when most species of sea turtles crawl out of the water to lay eggs. If the patrols spot a sea turtle making her way up the beach, they will follow her at a safe distance. Once the turtle starts to lay eggs, she doesn't seem to mind having an audience. When she returns to the water, volunteers can start the job of keeping the nest safe.

If the nest is in a protected spot, well above the high tide line, volunteers mark it and record the location. If the nest doesn't seem safe, they may carefully move the eggs to a place where they can hatch. Sometimes they will cover the nest with a mesh screen that keeps out predators like dogs and raccoons that would love to make a meal of turtle eggs.

After the baby turtles have had time to hatch and make their way down to the ocean, a scientist or a volunteer with special training comes back to check the nest, count the eggshells, and give any stragglers a boost. The hatchlings near the top of the nest get pushed out by those on the bottom, but the ones on the bottom sometimes have trouble making it out themselves. A gentle hand can make a difference.

Each nest that is protected and each hatchling that is saved give sea turtles a better chance of survival.

## Melati and Isabel Wijsen

When Melati Wijsen was twelve and her sister Isabel was ten, they learned in school how activists like Martin Luther King Jr. and Mahatma

Gandhi used peaceful protest to create a more just world. They decided that they wanted to do something to change the world too.

The Wijsen sisters grew up in Bali, in a home surrounded by rice fields, a short walk from the ocean. They were used to seeing plastic trash everywhere, and the problem was especially bad during Bali's rainy season. That's when storms at sea have been washing heaps of plastic up onto the beaches.

"There's no escaping it here," Melati told a reporter. "The plastic problem is so in your face, and we thought: 'Well, who's going to do something about it?'"

Melati and Isabel began by posting an online petition, asking Bali's government to ban single-use plastic bags. These bags, which mostly get thrown away after being used one time, are a huge source of plastic waste. As you already know, they are particularly dangerous for leatherback sea turtles, who see them floating in the water and mistake them for jellyfish.

The two sisters did not stop there.

They founded a group called Bye Bye Plastic Bags, contacted store owners and asked them to reduce the amount of plastic their stores used, and organized a regular event called Bali's Biggest Clean-Up. Year after year, volunteers gather on this day to remove trash, especially plastic trash, from Bali's beaches.

Keeping the beaches clean means less plastic washing out to sea, where it is a danger to marine animals like sea turtles. But Melati and Isabel did not forget that it would be even better if the plastic trash never landed on beaches in the first place.

Their online petition to get rid of single-use plastic bags in Bali gathered more than a hundred thousand signatures. But still the government of Bali did not take action. Melati and Isabel decided to draw more attention to the issue by doing something that Mahatma Gandhi had done—they went on a hunger strike.

Gandhi went on several hunger strikes and fasts during his years-long effort to win India's freedom from the British government. Some of his fasts lasted for weeks.

Because Melati and Isabel were so young, they chose to fast only between sunrise and sunset. They also met with a dietician, a health-care worker who is an expert on food and nutrition, to be sure that they stayed healthy.

Less than twenty-four hours after the sisters

started their hunger strike, the governor of Bali met with them. He signed a law banning plastic bags, plastic straws, and Styrofoam in Bali.

Melati has spoken at the United Nations and other worldwide organizations about the work she and her sister have done. At the age of nineteen, she founded a new organization

*Plastic trash like this on a beach in Bali is what drove Melati and Isabel Wijsen to action.*

called YOUTHTOPIA. Her focus is to create events and online tutorials to teach other young activists how to change the world for the better.

As Isabel once told a reporter, "Us kids may only be twenty-five percent of the world's population, but we are one hundred percent of the future."

As Melati and Isabel show, you're never too young to take action that can make the world better for others—including turtles. Supporting safe places for injured or endangered animals, making sure nests are protected, and keeping oceans clean are good ways to start. In a few pages, you'll find some other ways that you can help make sure that turtles will stay a part of the world we all share.

# FUN FACTS ABOUT TURTLES

1. Scientists sometimes use the name "chelonian" to refer to all turtles and tortoises as a group. *Chelonia* is the Greek word for *tortoise*.

2. There were turtles living alongside the dinosaurs. They survived the events that drove their giant reptile relatives to extinction.

3. Turtles have lungs that they use for breathing just like you do. But some species can also breathe a second way. A turtle has a single hole under its tail called

a cloaca. Waste and eggs both come out of this hole. And if they're spending a lot of time underwater, some turtles can suck water up inside the cloaca. Oxygen that is dissolved in the water enters the turtle's body this way. So these turtles actually breathe through their butts!

4. The deepest known dive ever made by a turtle is 3,937 feet. It was a leatherback sea turtle that set this record.

5. The term for the bottom half of a turtle's shell, the plastron, is also the word for the protective plate worn by a medieval knight under chain mail. (Nobody knows exactly where the term "carapace" came from.)

6. A desert tortoise can carry urine in its bladder for months. Since urine is

mostly water, the tortoise's body can use that water if it needs it to survive.

7. Green sea turtles eat mostly seaweed and algae. This gives their cartilage and fat a greenish color, which is how they got their name. (Their shells are not green.)

8. Kemp's ridley sea turtles are the only species of sea turtle that come ashore to build nests during the day. All other sea turtle species nest at night.

9. Turtles make noise. You already know that some hiss when they pull their heads back into their shells. Others grunt, chirp, squeak, or even roar. They may also make other sounds that human ears can't hear.

10. The largest known turtle of modern times was a leatherback whose body

washed up on the shores of Wales in 1988. It weighed two thousand pounds and was estimated to be around a hundred years old. Sadly, it drowned when it became entangled in fishing line. Its body is now on display in the National Museum Cardiff.

11. A group of turtles is called a bale (just like a group of whales is a pod, a group of horses is a herd, and a group of monkeys is a troop).

12. "Galapagos" is a Spanish word for tortoise. The Galapagos Islands were named after the giant tortoises that live there. So, yes, a Galapagos tortoise is a "tortoise tortoise."

13. *Terrapin* is another word for *turtle*. It usually describes a species that spends

some time on land and some in water. It is taken from one of the Algonquian languages of North America.

**14.** The first three human beings to orbit the moon were Frank Borman, Jim Lovell, and William Anders. They made their historic spaceflight in 1968. But they weren't the first earthlings to make it that far. Earlier the same year, the Soviet Union launched a spacecraft called Zond 5, which went around the moon and made it back to Earth. Zond 5 carried two tortoises. The spacecraft had a rough landing, splashing down in the Indian Ocean instead of landing in Kazakhstan as planned. But the tortoises were fine, except that they had lost a little weight during their trip.

# HOW YOU CAN HELP SAVE THE TURTLES

1.  Be sure to recycle any plastic bottles, cups, jars, and containers that you use. This keeps plastic out of trash cans and landfills where it can end up in the ocean or waterways.

2.  Even better than recycling plastic is not to use it in the first place. Take a look at how many times you use something plastic in an average day and try to come up with ways to use less of it. Can you drink from a refillable water bottle instead of a plastic bottle that gets tossed

after one use? Can you bring a cloth bag to the store instead of using a plastic bag? Can you use a cloth bag or metal container for your sandwich at lunch?

3. Never bring a wild turtle home as a pet. If you want to own a turtle, ask an adult to help you find a good pet store and ask to be sure that the turtles sold there were not captured in the wild.

4. Never set a pet turtle loose into the wild. A pet animal isn't likely to survive on its own, and it can also spread disease to other wild reptiles.

5. Leave leaf litter and broken branches on the forest floor. Turtles and other small animals rely on this material to stay hidden from predators and as cover from hot sun or chilly wind. If you live in a

house with a yard, ask your parents if you can pick a corner where leaves and branches can stay on the ground.

6. If you're in a car, ask the driver to follow the speed limit. It's common for turtles to be hit by speeding cars.

7. If you see a turtle crossing the road and there are no other cars in sight, let it make its own way. If there is a lot of traffic and you think the turtle might be in danger, ask an adult to help move it safely to the side of the road where it was headed. (Turtles are usually crossing a road for a reason, maybe to reach food or water. If you bring them back where they started, they will just try to cross the road again.)

8. If you're out in the desert and spot a

desert tortoise crossing the road, be extra careful about moving it. Desert tortoises tend to pee when they are frightened or startled (which might be the case if someone picks them up). This can be a real problem for a tortoise in a desert—they can't afford to lose any water. You can learn more about picking up a desert tortoise safely here: NPS.gov/jotr/learn/nature/tortoise.htm

9. If you're hiking or walking anywhere in the wilderness, and especially around an ocean, lake, river, or pond, be careful to bring all your trash home with you. Don't leave anything where it can harm wild animals like turtles.

10. If you live near a beach, join a volunteer beach-cleaning day. Keeping beaches

clean means less trash in the ocean to endanger sea turtles and other marine creatures. Get your friends, family, scout troop, or other group to come along and help clean the beaches too. The more people who help, the better for turtles!

11. If you're visiting a beach where sea turtles are known to nest, fill in deep holes and knock down sandcastles before you go home. They can block sea turtles trying to make their way up the beach to lay eggs.

12. Don't set helium balloons loose. They look pretty sailing away, but they have to come down somewhere. If they end up lakes, rivers, streams, or the ocean, they are dangerous for turtles and other water-dwelling creatures.

**13.** When you are old enough to vote, choose leaders who care about the environment and will work to protect animals like turtles. Right now, talk to the adults in your life and encourage them to vote for a safer world for all wild creatures.

**14.** Read books and visit zoos and aquariums to learn more about turtles. (Visit AZA.org to see if the place you want to visit has been approved by the Association of Zoos and Aquariums. This means the animals there get good care.) Share what you learn with others and encourage them to make the world better for turtles and all wild animals. Here are a few books to get you started:

*The Book of Turtles*
by Sy Montgomery

*Diego, the Galapagos Giant Tortoise:*
*Saving a Species from Extinction*
by Darcy Pattison

*Turtles of the World:*
*A Guide to Every Family*
by Jeffrey E. Lovich

# REFERENCES

Baker, Harry. "Can Turtles Really Breathe
Through Their Butts?" LiveScience:
Animals, July 31, 2022. livescience.com
/can-turtles-breathe-through-butts.

Bittel, Jason. "Extinction Threatens More than
Half of the World's Turtles and Tortoises."
Natural Resources Defense Council,
July 21, 2020. nrdc.org/stories/extinction
-threatens-more-half-worlds-turtles-and
-tortoises.

Casey, Nicholas. "Meet Diego, the Centenarian
Whose Sex Drive Saved His Species."

*The New York Times*, March 11, 2017.
nytimes.com/2017/03/11/world/americas
/galapagos-islands-tortoises.html.

Charles Darwin Foundation. "About Us."
Accessed December 21, 2022.
darwinfoundation.org/en/about.

Fortin, Jacey. "Once Threatened, Sea Turtle
Nests Thrive Along Georgia Coasts."
*The New York Times*, June 13, 2019.
nytimes.com/2019/06/13/science
/sea-turtles-georgia.html.

Free, Cathy. "The World's Oldest Living Land
Animal? At Age 190, It's Jonathan the
Tortoise." *The Washington Post*, January
30, 2022. washingtonpost.com/lifestyle
/2022/01/31/oldest-animal-tortoise
-jonathan-/.

Galapagos Conservation Trust. "Galapagos

Giant Tortoise." Accessed December 7,
2022. galapagosconservation.org.uk
/wildlife/galapagos-giant-tortoise/.

Gilchrist, Karen. "She Got Plastic Bags
Banned on Bali by 18. Now She Wants to
Mobilize Other Young Activists." CNBC
Make It, August 20, 2020. cnbc.com/2020
/08/20/plastic-pollution-gen-z-activist
-melati-wijsen-mobilizes-others.html.

National Geographic. "Animals: Photo Ark:
Leatherback Sea Turtle." Photographs by
Joel Sartore. Accessed December 7, 2022.
nationalgeographic.com/animals/reptiles
/facts/leatherback-sea-turtle?rnd=
1686622554292&loggedin=true.

NOAA Fisheries. "10 Tremendous Turtle
Facts." June 15, 2020. fisheries.noaa.gov
/feature-story/10-tremendous-turtle-facts.

NOAA Fisheries. "What Can You Do to Save Sea Turtles?" June 8, 2022. fisheries.noaa .gov/feature-story/what-can-you-do-save -sea-turtles.

NPS/Lian Law. "When and How to Move a Tortoise." National Park Service, June 21, 2015. Accessed December 7, 2022. Video, 3:59. nps.gov/media/video/view.htm?id =0C4DAD93-1DD8-B71B-0B16FB- 6CA5649F09.

Paddock, Richard C. "After Fighting Plastic in 'Paradise Lost,' Sisters Take on Climate Change." *The New York Times*, July 3, 2020. nytimes.com/2020/07/03/world /asia/bali-sisters-plastic-climate-change .html.

Roth, Annie. "He wants the 'homeland of the turtle' to lead in conserving the species."

*National Geographic*, January 8, 2021.
nationalgeographic.com/magazine
/article/tomas-diagne-wants-africa-to-lead
-in-turtle-conservation?loggedin=true&rnd
=1671475931473.

San Diego Zoo Wildlife Alliance. "Turtle and Tortoise." San Diego Zoo Wildlife Alliance Animals & Plants. Accessed December 5, 2022. animals.sandiegozoo.org/animals /turtle-and-tortoise.

San Diego Zoo Wildlife Alliance. "Galapagos Tortoise." San Diego Zoo Wildlife Alliance Animals & Plants. Accessed December 18, 2022. animals.sandiegozoo.org/animals /galapagos-tortoise.

Smithsonian's National Zoo & Conservation Biology Institute. "Eastern Box Turtle."

Animals A-Z. Accessed December 8, 2022. nationalzoo.si.edu/animals/eastern -box-turtle.

World Wildlife Fund. "Sea Turtles." Our Work: Species. Accessed December 6, 2022. worldwildlife.org/species/sea-turtle.

**SARAH L. THOMSON** has published more than thirty books, including prose and poetry, fiction and non-fiction, picture books, and novels. Her work includes two adventures featuring a teenage girl ninja, a riveting survival story about wildfires and wombats, and nonfiction about elephants, sharks, tigers, plesiosaurs, saber-toothed cats, and other fascinating creatures. *School Library Journal* called Sarah's picture book *Cub's Big World* "a big must-have." *The Bulletin of the Center for Children's Books* described her novel *Deadly Flowers* as "clever, dangerous, vivacious," and *Booklist* said this fantasy set in feudal Japan is "genuinely thrilling, with surprises at every turn and a solid emotional core." *Deadly Flowers* also received Wisconsin's Elizabeth Burr/Worzalla award. Sarah worked as an editor at HarperCollins and Simon & Schuster before becoming a full-time writer. She lives in Portland, Maine.

Learn more about her work at
SarahLThomson.com.

**CHELSEA CLINTON** is the author of the #1 *New York Times* bestseller *She Persisted: 13 American Women Who Changed the World*; *She Persisted Around the World: 13 Women Who Changed History*; *She Persisted in Sports: American Olympians Who Changed the Game*; *She Persisted in Science: Brilliant Women Who Made a Difference*; *Don't Let Them Disappear: 12 Endangered Species Across the Globe*; *Welcome to the Big Kids Club*; *It's Your World: Get Informed, Get Inspired & Get Going!*; *Start Now!: You Can Make a Difference*; with Hillary Clinton, *Grandma's Gardens* and *The Book of Gutsy Women: Favorite Stories of Courage and Resilience*; and, with Devi Sridhar, *Governing Global Health: Who Runs the World and Why?* She is also the Vice Chair of the Clinton Foundation, where she works on many initiatives, including those that help empower the next generation of leaders. She lives in New York City with her husband, Marc, and their children.

You can follow Chelsea Clinton on Twitter
@ChelseaClinton
or on Facebook at
Facebook.com/ChelseaClinton

# DON'T MISS MORE BOOKS IN THE

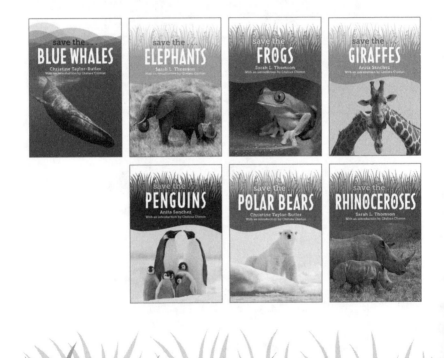

# save the ... SERIES!